DORAEMON

Gadget Cat from the Future

VOLUME 8

ドラえもん

Fujiko F. Fujio
PRESENTS

I messed up!

I was a little confused!

A cat-shaped robot
born on September 3, 2112.
He rode a time machine all the way back from
the 22nd century to help Nobita.
He can pull all sorts of secret tools out of
the "4-D(Fourth Dimensional) Pocket"
on his tummy whenever Nobita needs them
to get himself out of trouble.

藤子・F・不二雄

Contents
もくじ

Guide to the Book
この本の読み方

「コチョコチョ」の英訳。効果音や叫び声、おどろきの声などは、アメリカのまんが的な表現を使用したり、音のひびきを英語で表したりして、ふん囲気を出しています。英語辞書にのっていないものも、あります。

ドラえもんのひみつ道具は、日本語部分では「 」（かぎかっこ）をつけています。

TICKLE TICKLE

「マジックおなか」をくすぐる.

Tickle the "Magic *Onaka*."

ドラえもんのひみつ道具は、英語部分では""（クオーテーションマーク）で表しています。原則として、ひみつ道具は斜体のローマ字で表していますが、外来語として定着している単語（マジック、カメラ、ポケットなど）は、そのまま英語で表示しました。

効果音やおどろきの声は絵としてあつかっていますので、そのまま訳さずのせています。

原作のまんがに合わせ、右開きですので、ふきだしは、右から左へと読んでください。てんとう虫コミックス「ドラえもん」のまんがのセリフを訳としてつけてあります。

ドラえもんのまんがのセリフを英訳。特に意味を重視しながら訳しているので、原文には出てこない単語が英訳に出てくる場合があります。

やめて.　　苦しい！

Stop!

I can't stand it!

WA HA WA HA　　**HA HA HA HA**

"Honnin Video"

本人ビデオ

8

CLICK

カチ

ほめられた時間は？
場所は？

What time did he say it and where?

「本人ビデオ」

"Honnin Video."

ドタ バタ ドタ

Because we're far from school.

Nothing is happening.

THUD THUD THUD

学校から、
遠いからね.

なんにもおこらない.

ワッ，先生!!

Yikes, teacher!!

ビデオテープみたいに，本人が
同じことやってみせるんだ.

？

The person himself will do the same thing over, just like in a video.

？

えらい！きみが，そんなまじめな
子だとは，しらなかった.

Good for you! I didn't know you were such a hard-working boy.

9

10

11

調べてみましょう. 時間を,
ぎゃくもどりさせていけばいい.

Let's check.
Just make the clock
go backwards.

ママのくつをしらない?
げんかんから, きえちゃったのよ.

Have you seen my
shoes? They
disappeared from
our entrance hall.

TROT　　TROT

ヒョコ

5分前. 10分前. 15分前.

5
minutes
earlier,

10 minutes
earlier,

15 minutes
earlier.

どうもありがとう.

Thank you
very much.

このイヌだったのか.

So it was
the dog!

みよう.

Let's
see it.

へえ,
みたかったな.

Wow,
I sure
wanted to
see that.

ジャイアンがさ,
あきかんですべって
ひっくり返って.

Gian slipped
on an empty
can and fell
over.

どうしたの.

What's
up?

クスクス…….

Giggle,
giggle...

12

THUMP

DASH ... なるほど，2人とも走ってきたのか． ... **DASH**

So, they both came running.

ええとね
....

どっちが悪かった？

BANG

Well...

Which one was it?

う～ん…，
まだわからない．

BANG

速すぎて，よくわかんなかった．
もういっぺんみせて．

Hmm... I still can't figure it out.

It was too fast I couldn't make out. Let me see it again.

BANG ... もういっぺん．

BANG ... もういっぺん．

Again.

Again.

14

"Mohan Tegami Pen"

もはん手紙ペン

18

20

21

rush to your place and,

the postman will,

If you put this stamp on,

deliver it directly in a big hurry.

直接大急ぎでとどけてくれるんだ．

どうしたの!?　　　　　　まあ….　　あら….　　　　　のび太さんから？

What's the matter!?

My...

Oh...

From Nobita-san?

のび太さん!!　　　　　　ほんと!?　　しずちゃんが，
走ってくる．

Nobita-san!!

Really !?

Shizu-chan is running over.

22

あ，ごめんなさい.

Oh, I'm sorry.

やあ，さっきはどうしたの？急にかけだして.

Hey. What happened back there, running off all of a sudden?

....

....

じゃ….

Bye.

じゃあね.

Bye.

なるほど…，手紙と本人の差がひらきすぎて，かえって印象を悪くしたのか.

I see..., the gap between the letter and the real writer was too big, so it made a bad impression.

ずっとペンを使い続けるしかないよ.

You'll just have to keep using the pen.

でも，あって話せばまたけいべつされる.

もういっぺんかすよ.

But if I talk to her in person she'll think I'm rotten again.

I'll let you use it again.

24

「かくこととしゃべることが
　ちがいすぎてはずかしい
　のですが，でも…」

のび太さんて，
かくこととしゃべることが
ちがいすぎるんだもの.

またお手紙？

"I'm ashamed that what I write and what I say are too different, but..."

What you write and what you say are too different.

A letter again?

Don't say anything!

Let's have a talk.

しゃべるんじゃ
ないぞ.

ゆっくりお話し
したいわ.

SOB SOB
OVERWHELMED

SHOCK

これからあとどうしたら
いいかしらね.

早く
続きをかいて.

まあ…,
なんて美しいことば….

Now what are we going to do?

Hurry, write more.

My! What lovely words...

The Invincible "Seigi Rope"

おそるべき正義ロープ

SMACK

すぐほどけっ. やいこら.

Untie me now.

Hey you.

つみが重くなると，しばられ方も，
ひどくなるんだ.

The bigger the sin,
the tighter it ties you up.

雨….

DROP

Rain
...

これからは，「正義ロープ」が
町の平和を守ってくれるだろう.

From now on, the "*Seigi*" Rope"
will keep peace in this town.

SLIP

PATTER PATTER

WRIGGLE WRIGGLE

RAIN RAIN

どうぞどうぞ.

Come in.

どこかで
雨やどりしよう.

Let's get out of the rain.

しずちゃん, ピアノの
レッスンのお時間よ.

Shizu-chan, time for your piano lesson.

こっちがもっと
おもしろいわよ.

This one's even funnier.

この本,
おもしろいね.

This book is funny.

SUDDENLY

うそ
ついたの.

You lied.

ピアノの先生,
きびしいからきらい.

I hate my piano teacher, because she's so mean.

おなかが
いたいから, 休むわ.

I'm not going, because I have a stomach-ache.

33

ロープが
うようよでたらしい.

PTUI

It seems the Ropes are swarming everywhere.

たいへんなことになった.

We're in trouble.

SUDDENLY

ニュウ

"Keep Out"

立入禁止
はいるな

近道して急ごう.

Let's hurry and take a short cut.

34

もとのタネにもどるんだ.

They'll return to seed form.

CLICK

カチ

"Rope *Yobimodoshi* Button."

よ, よしっ.

O, okay.

早く「正義ロープ」を.

The *Seigi Rope*. Hurry.

よくもやったなっ.

I'm going to get you.

まずい！
ここじゃ使えないよう.

No! We can't use it here.

"Keep Off The Grass"

"Ozashiki Suizokukan"

おざしき水族館

いくら口で
いってもむだだ。

いや、この話は
もうよそう。

I just
can't
express it
in words.

Well,
I should
stop now.

窓の外を泳いでいく魚たち
のゆめのような美しさ…….

The beauty of fish
swimming outside
that window, it's like
a dream.

厚いガラスばり
の展望室に
なっていて,

It's an
observation
room
surrounded
by thick
glass.

エレベーターを
おりると、そこは
もう海の底だ.

Once you
get off the
elevator,
you're at
the bottom
of the sea.

The wonder of the Marine
Park is something you
have to experience to
understand.

海中公園のすばらしさは、いって
みた者じゃないとわからないよ.

うらやましい.

I am
jealous.

しかし….

But
...

だれがうらや
ましがるか!!

Who cares
about some
park!!

うらやまし
がらせようと
思って.

He's just
trying to
make us
jealous.

わからない
話なら、はじめ
からするな!!

If it's something
we can't
understand, then
don't talk about it
in the first place.

楽しみに、
まってるからねえ.

We're
looking
forward
to it.

ドラえもんも、
めんどくさがり
だからなあ.

But
Doraemon's
kind of a
lazy guy,
you know.

つれてって
もらいま
しょうよ.

See if he'll
take us
there.

そうだ!!
ドラえもんに
たのんで,

I know!!
Let's ask
Doraemon
and...

PING PING

ピコン
ピコン

昼寝か. めずらしい.

He's taking a nap? It's not like him.

「どこでもドア」さえ かしてもらえれば.

All I need to do is to borrow the "*Dokodemo* Door".

おこさなくても いいんだ.

There's no need to wake him up.

そうだ!!

I know !!

しっぽがピコピコしてるのは, きげんの悪いしょうこだ.

That tail means he's not in a good mood.

「スモールライト」 関係ない.

"Small Light", not this either.

関係ないや. 「声カタマリン」 か.

Don't need that.

The "*Koe Katamarin*".

なんだこりゃ!?

What the heck!?

関係ないもの ばかりでてくる.

I don't need any of these.

「おざしきつりぼり」

"*Ozashiki Tsuribori*."

「手ばり」

"*Te-bari*."

40

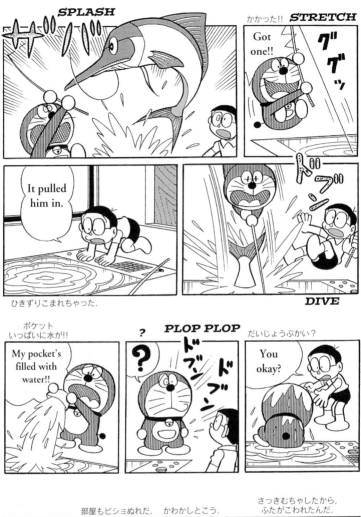

SPLASH

STRETCH
かかった!!

Got one!!

It pulled him in.

ひきずりこまれちゃった.

DIVE

ポケット
いっぱいに水が!!

My pocket's filled with water!!

?

PLOP PLOP

だいじょうぶかい?

You okay?

部屋もビショぬれだ. かわかしとこう.

The room is soaked too.

I'll let it dry.

さっきむちゃしたから,
ふたがこわれたんだ.

The lid broke, because you forced it earlier.

41

42

すごいすごい. ほうら，魚でいっぱい.

ほんとの海底公園へいっても，
こんなのみられないね.

みて!!
いってみよう. あれ，クジラじゃない!?

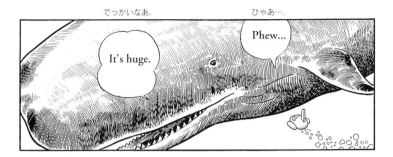

46

ケテスタだって.

It says, "L-P-E-H".

なんか文字が
うかんでる.

There's some letters floating.

あがって
まってて.

Why don't you wait inside.

いま,
いないのよ.

He's not here right now.

おもしろくないっ.

No fun.

帰ろ帰ろ,
ばからしい.

Let's go home. This is ridiculous.

２人だけで
いっちゃったのかしら.

I wonder if they went without us.

どこへいった
のかしら….

Where can they be...

はずみで,
もとにもどれた.

We got back to our proper size by accident.

"Wasuremono Okuritodoke-ki"

忘れ物おくりとどけ機

忘れてきた.　　　　しまった.

I forgot it.

Oh no!

宿題を集めます.

Let's collect your homework.

まず, ボールか.

First, a ball, huh?

まず, ボールをだすよ.

First, I'll make a ball appear.

どこかに, かくしてたんだ. もっと大きな物, だしてみろ.

You must've had it hidden somewhere. Show us something bigger.

わあ, じょうずね.

Wow, you're good.

はあい.

Here you go.

ROLL

コロン

花びんか, よしきた.

A vase. Got it.

よし, 花びんをだそう.

Okay, a vase then.

だすよ.

Yes, I can.

花をだしてみせろ. だせないだろう.

Show us a flower. I bet you can't do that.

ひゃあ.

Phew.

THUD THUD

ドサ ドサ

Someone Worse Than Me Came To Class

ぼくよりダメなやつがきた

He runs slower than me, and of course can't do flips or pull-ups and...

But this kid, he gets a zero 3 times out of 10. Ha-ha-ha.

I get a zero in about every 5 tests, right?

This is so great! There is someone in this world who is worse than me!!

Hey, come on in.

Tame-kun's here!!

Is Nobita-kun home?

Yeah.

We promised to do homework together.

61

63

64

てんとう虫コミックス「ドラえもん」第23巻 収録作品

Sweets
Ranch

おかし牧場

MOO   MOO

70

NEIGH   BAA BAA   MOO

A Popular Guy With The "Medachi Light"

めだちライトで人気者

79

80

うるさいな. いって
みなけりゃわかんない.

Shut up.
I won't know
until I get
there.

だれに試すの？ 試してどう
するの？ 何時ごろ帰る？

Who are you testing it on? What
happens after you test it? When
will you come home?

こんな熱い視線を感じた
こと, はじめてだよ.

I've never felt anyone
stare at me like this
before.

They're
into some
silly
game.

くだらない遊びに
夢中になってる.

のび太がきた.

Nobita's
here.

のび太だ!!

It's
Nobita!!

あらっ,
のび太さん.

Oh,
Nobita-san.

83

84

いくいく！
つれてって.

Yes, yes! Take me with you.

海をみにいくの,
いっしょにくる?

I'm going to see the ocean. Do you want to come with me?

スミレさんは, ぼくの
ことうるさくきいたり
しないんだね.

You don't seem to ask me so many questions.

人けのない海って
大すき.

SPLASH   SPLASH

I love the ocean when there aren't any people around.

Because I myself am always being chased around.

自分がいつも,
おいまわされてるから.

ときどきひとり
きりになりたく
なるのよ.

But sometimes I feel like being all alone.

ま, こういうお仕事
してればしかたのない
ことなんだけどね….

Well, I guess you can't help it when you're in this sort of business...

86

すぐにわかるよ.

> You'll find out soon.

な, なにを したんだ!?

> Wh, what did you do!?

FLASH

ピカ

本物だ!!

> The real thing!!

そうだ, あの人だ.

> Yes, it's that guy.

テレビにでてる レポーターの.

> The reporter on TV.

あんたは もしや.

> You are perhaps?

とうぶんにげまわるから スミレさんとこへ こられないと思うよ.

> He'll be running for quite a while, so I don't think he will come to you.

How To Enjoy The Gian Recital

ジャイアンリサイタルを楽しむ方法

89

94

ほ，ほ，本気で
いってるのか!?

アンコール
アンコール.

もう？
もっと
きかせてよ.

そろそろ
お別れの….

ファンのご声援にささ
えられ，2時間はゆめ
のようにすぎました.

A, are you guys serious!?

Encore, encore.

Already? Let us hear more.

My last song will be...

Thanks to support from fans, my two hours have passed like a dream.

そ，そんなにも
おれの歌を….

J, just for my singing...

あした続きを
やるから.

かんべん
してくれよう.

そんなことで
プロになれるか.

根性がないぞ!!

もう声が
かれて….

のどが
…….

I'll do another show tomorrow.

Take it easy, guys.

And you think you can become a pro?

Don't you have any guts!?

I'm getting hoarse...

My throat...

約束忘れるな!!

きっと.

きっとだね.

Don't forget your promise!!

For sure.

For sure?

?

It was a pleasant day.

I bet it was a disaster.

So he's finished at last.

Let's make dad addicted to chewing gum.

These are good pills.

With this pill.

Just try one piece.

I hate gum.

I get it! He can quit smoking.

Since you can't smoke while chewing gum...

Gum is really good!

SQUISH CHEW
SQUISH CHEW

Nobita Runs Away for a Long Time

のび太のなが～い家出

だれがこんな家に！

でていくとも!!

Who wants to live in this house anyway!

I will get out!!

でていきなさい!!

あんたなんかもう、うちの子じゃありません!!

Get out!!

You're no longer my child!

いくら親でも、あんなひどいこといっていいものだろうか.

Even if she is my mother, she can't say such terrible things to me.

ずっとがまんしてたが、も～たくさんだ!!

I've put up with her for a long time, but this is just too much!!

とめるな!!

Don't try to stop me!

忘れないよ.

きみには世話になった.

I won't forget you.

Thanks for all you've done for me.

ぼくがかけがえのないひとりむすこだってことを….

She'll see that I'm her precious, one and only son.

ぼくがいなくなったら、思いしるだろう.

When I'm gone, then she'll see.

101

楽しいことを時間をたっぷりかけて味わう
ための機械なんだ. 光をあびると,
10分が1時間に感じられる.

This is a device for taking plenty of time to enjoy fun things. When you're hit with the ray, ten minutes feels like an hour.

「時間ナガナガ光線」

"Jikan Naga-naga Kou-sen."

ま, いいかげんに
帰ってきな.

Ok, come back when you feel like it.

FLASH

…ところで,
どこへいこう.

...by the way, where should I go?

これからどこへいって
なにをしてもいいんだ.

From now on I can go wherever I want and do whatever I want.

ああっ, 自由って
いいなあ.

Aah, freedom sure is great.

よくやった!!おまえに
そんな勇気があるとは
思わなかったぜ.

Good job! I didn't think you had it in you!

えらい!!

That's great!!

なにっ, 家出!?

What, are you running away from home?

おう, どこへいくんだ.

Hey, where are you going?

103

104

105

107

どんなに
しかられるかなあ.

I wonder how much she's going to scold me.

えっ, そんなに
心配してるのか.

Huh, is she really that worried?

ごめんなさい.

I'm sorry.

神さま, のび太をお返しください. ぶじに帰って
さえくれたら………, 神さま.

God, please bring Nobita back to me. God, if he just comes back unhurt...

のび太が３時間ぶりに
帰ってきたの.

Nobita's come home after three hours.

なにがあったんだい？

What happened?

Jaiko, Comic Book Artist

まんが家ジャイ子

ばかみたい.

You're being silly.

WA HA HA HA WA HA HA HA HA

いかにも
わざとらしい.

It still sounds forced.

どう？

How's that?

**WA HA HA
WA HA HA**

えっ, ジャイ子がギャグまんがを？
うまくわらわないと, なぐられる？

What? Jaiko is writing comic strips? If you don't laugh properly, you'll get beat up?

「マジックおなか」

"Magic *Onaka.*"

じゃ, わらわ
せてやろう.

Ok, I'll make you laugh.

こっちへつける.

Stick it here.

へそをはずして…,

Take off the belly button …

おなかだして.

Show me your tummy.

114

115

116

MOVED

"Kanzume Can" Comics
カンヅメカンでまんがを

おもしろそう
じゃない.

へえ, みんなでまんが
雑誌を作るの.

That sounds like fun.

What? You're all making a comic book magazine?

弱ったなあ….

Now what do I do...

まんが家じゃないんだから, へ
たならへたなりに, いっしょう
けんめいかいた作品なら….

You're not a comic book artist, so even if it's bad, as long as you tried your best...

じゃ, それを
わたせばいいのに.

Well then you could have just handed it in.

かいたことは
かいたんだよ.

I did draw it.

しめきりは守らなくちゃ
いけないよ, みんなに
迷惑をかけるから.

You've got to make the deadline or you'll annoy everyone.

わあ, はっきりいって
くれちゃって.

Boo hoo, it's true...

それにしても, これは
へたくそすぎるなあ.

But this is really too awful.

………………

......

じ〜っと念力を注ぐと, かき
たい絵がうかんでくるんだ.

If you stare at this paper with all your might, the picture you want to draw will appear.

「念画紙」

"Nenga-shi."

130

ほんとの画家が
かいたみたい！

うまい！

It really looks
like a pro
drew it!

That's
great!

よけいなことを考えると，
絵にまざるから．

まじめに考
えるんだぞ．

ＳＦまんがを頭にうかべれば，
そのとおりにかけるんだね．

If you think of something
else it will get mixed up
in your picture.

Think
seriously.

If I think of a scifi comic
book story, I can draw
it just like that.

ああ，まずい！

お使いに
いってきて．

タイトルページは，かっこ
よくロケットがとんでいる
ところ……．

Oh no!

Go run
an
errand.

On the title page,
there's a cool picture
of a rocket in flight...

133

134

The Night Before Nobita's Wedding

のび太の結婚前夜

138

未来のぼくだ!!

It's me in the future!

SCREECH

どちらさまの，ご婚礼でございますか

式場はどこでしょう．

May I have the name of the bride and groom, please?

ATION

Where is the ceremony?

ちこくしそうになったんだろ．

大あわてでかけこんでいったよ．

You looked like you were late.

I was in a big hurry.

いくつになってもしようがないなあ．

1日かんちがいしてたんだ．

No matter how old you get, you're still hopeless.

I was off by a whole day.

野比のび太さまと，源静香さまのお式は，あすの予定になっておりますが……．

The ceremony for Nobi Nobita and Minamoto Shizuka is scheduled for tomorrow...

And you called me hopeless!!

I pressed the wrong button on the "Time Machine."

Wait... If the ceremony is tomorrow, why did we come here?

人のこといえないだろ!!

「タイムマシン」のボタンをおしまちがえた．

まてよ……．式があすなら，ぼくらはどうしてここへきたの？

しずちゃんは, どうしてるかな.

I wonder what Shizu-chan is doing?

つきあいきれない. もう夜中だよ.

The party still isn't over but we can't stay.

It's already midnight.

心配だ. みてくる.

おい, よせよ!

ひょっとしてかるはずみな婚約をくやんでないてるかも……

She isn't by any chance crying because she regrets that she got engaged without thinking it through, is she?

Hey, cut it out!

I'm worried. Let's go look.

親子3人でお別れパーティーをやったらしい.

It looks like she's having a farewell party with her parents, just the three of them.

お父さんにおやすみのごあいさつをして.

Go say good night to your father.

はい.

あとかたづけはいいから, おやすみなさい. あすは早いのよ.

Yes.

You don't have to help clean up. Just go to bed. You have to get up early tomorrow.

142

143

「正直電波」

"Shoujiki Denpa."

かえって話せないものだよ. こんなときには……

All the more reason she can't talk to him. At times like this...

あれだけ？あすはおよめにいくってのに少しぐらい話があってもよさそうなもんだ.

That's it? If she's getting married tomorrow, it seems like she should talk to him a little more.

パパ!!

Daddy!!

思ってることなんでもしゃべらずにいられなくなるんだ. ふつうならてれくさくていえないようなことまでも.

This lets you say all the things you're thinking. Even things you're too shy to mention.

なんでなんで!?

ええっ!!

Why not!?

What!!

パパ! あたし, およめにいくのやめる!!

Daddy! I'm not going to get married!!

そりゃもちろんだ.

あたしがいっちゃったらパパさびしくなるでしょ.

Well of course.

If I leave home, you'll be sad, won't you, Daddy?

なんかへやの中がさわがしい…….

It's noisy in here...

144

とんでもない. きみはぼくらに
すばらしいおくり物を残して
いってくれるんだよ.

それなのにあたしのほうは,
パパやママになんにもして
あげられなかったわ.

これまでずうっと甘えたり
わがままいったり…,

Nonsense. You have left us with wonderful gifts.

I've never done anything for you and Mom.

I've been spoiled and selfish until now...

数えきれないほどのね.

そう.

おくり物？
あたしが？

More than we can count.

Yes.

Gifts? Me?

かすかに東の空が白んでは
いたが, 頭の上はまだ
一面の星空だった.

病院をでたとき,

最初のおくり物はきみがうまれて
きてくれたことだ.

there was a faint light in the eastern sky but above my head, the sky was filled with stars.

When we left the hospital

The first present was that you were born to us.

It was three o'clock in the morning. Your cries sounded like the trumpets of angels. I never heard such a happy sound.

午前３時ごろだったよ. きみの産声が天使
のラッパみたいにきこえた. あんなに美し
い音楽はきいたことがない.

あの青年は人のしあわせを願い，人の不幸を
悲しむことのできる人だ．それがいちばん
人間にとってだいじなことなんだからね．

He is the kind of person who wants others to be happy, and feels bad about others' unhappiness. That's the most important quality for a person to have.

のび太くんを選んだきみの
判断は正しかったと思うよ.

I think your judgment in choosing Nobita is correct.

I believe without doubt that he will make you happy.

かれなら，まちがいなくきみをしあわせに
してくれるとぼくは信じているよ.

きっときっと，きみをしあわせに
してみせるからね!!

I promise, I promise I'll make you happy!!

英語力を高める
ワンポイントレッスン

このコミックでは、わかりやすい単語だけでなく、ふだんよく使われる英語表現を選んで使用しています。このコーナーでは、さらに英語の理解を深めるため、いくつかの英語表現について例をあげてご説明します。

10ページ3段目

どうもどうも.

Hi there.は、「やあ」「どうも」とばくぜんと呼びかけるときに用いる表現です。Hello there.とも言います。

13ページ3段目

なにを!!

なんだと!!

What the!!は、「なんだと!」とけんかをするときによく使われます。What the hell!!または、What the fuck!!という表現の、hellやfuckという汚い言葉を言わないようにしたものです。

149

かけつけてきて,　　郵便局の人が,

> rush to your place and,
>
> the postman will,

男性の郵便局員なので、-manという「男性」を意識させる要素を含んだpostmanを用いています。女性に対してpostmanと言うと差別的に感じられるため、一般的に「郵便配達の人」と言う場合は、男女の区別のないpostal carrierやmail carrierが好まれる傾向にあります。

許せない.　　正しい者がなかされて,　悪者がいばってる.

> I can't stand that.
>
> The one who's right ends up crying while the bad guy struts around.

strut aroundの文字通りの意味は、「いばって歩く」です。ここではこれを比ゆ的に使っています。またend up…は、「最後には…になる」という表現です。

どこかで雨やどりしよう.

> Let's get out of the rain.

「雨やどりをする」は、「避難、保護」の意味のshelterを使って、take [find, seek] shelter from the rainと言うこともできます。

33ページ2段目

このロープは
きびしいんだ.

あんな
うそぐらいで….

This rope is
strict, you
know.

It was just a
little white lie.

white lieは、「白いうそ」では何のことかわかりませんね。このwhiteは、「悪意のない、たわいのない、無害な」という意味です。「悪意のあるうそ」をblack lieと言うこともできます。

38ページ1段目

いくら口で
いってもむだだ.

いや、この話は
もうよそう.

I just
can't
express it
in words.

Well,
I should
stop now.

「口でいってもむだだ」という表現を、英語では「言葉では言い表せない」と解釈して訳しています。

45ページ3段目

やっと,
底についた.

CLUNK

We've
finally hit
the
bottom.

動詞のhitは、「たたく、衝突する」という意味でよく使われますが、絵を見るとそれほど勢いよく当たっているわけではありません。ここでのhitは、「…に到着する、着く」という意味の口語の用法です。

51ページ4段目

うつった.

There
we go.

There we go.は、「私たちはそこへ行く」ではありません。目の前で起こっていることに人の注意を引くときに使う決まり文句で、ここでは「よし、うまくいった」「ほら、このとおり」ぐらいの意味です。

52ページ2段目

きっとあのかさ,
忘れてくるよ.

にわか雨だから,
やんじゃったよ.

He'll probably
forget that
umbrella at
his office.

It was just a
shower, and
now it's
stopped.

日本語にもなっている「シャワー」ですが、英語のshowerは「にわか雨」の意味でもとてもよく使われます。場合によっては、「にわか雪」や「ちょっとの間ふるみぞれ[あられ]」をさすこともあります。

52ページ4段目

たねもしかけも
ありません.

Nothing
up my
sleeve.

英語では、Nothing up my sleeve.（そでの中にはなにも隠していません）を手品の前の決まり文句としてよく使います。もとは、トランプでだますために余分なカードをそでの中に隠し持っていたことからきています。

53ページ2段目

なんだい,あんな手品で
いばっちゃって.

Getting on his
high horse for
such a
cheap
trick.

high horseは、「いばった態度」を意味します。「いばるのをやめる」「謙虚になる」なら、get [come] off one's high horseと言うことができます。

58ページ1段目

けんすいもできないし…
もちろんさかあがりも
かけっこもぼくよりおそいし·

He runs slower than
me, and of course
can't do flips or pull-
ups and...

「さかあがり」に対する一般的な英語の表現は、ないようです。ここでは、flipという鉄棒での回転動作を表す語で代用しています。

68ページ2段目

草でかう?かえるもんか,
お金でなきゃ.

この草で
チョコをかうんだ.

Get with grass?
No, you can't.
You need
money.

You get
chocolates
from this
grass.

日本語は「飼う」を「買う」と誤解した会話です。英語では、「手に入れる」と「買う」の意味をもつgetを使い、「チョコレートを草からとるんだ」と言うドラえもんに対して、「草で買うだって?」とのび太が聞き返しています。

72ページ1段目

なるほど、 それも困るなあ.

あしたは1日じゅう頭がぼやあっとして…, 教室でいねむりして, おこられる.

You're right, that's a problem.

Tomorrow I'll be out of it for the whole day, and I'll fall asleep in class, and get scolded.

be out of itは、俗語で「頭がぼうっとしている」を表します。寝不足だけでなく、酒によっぱらっていることなどが原因の場合にも使われます。

74ページ3段目

みどりの牧草、明るい日ざし、 楽しく遊ぶおかしたち…, のどかな風景だなあ.

子チョコが チョコチョコと かわいいわ.

いろんな おかしがずいぶん ふえたなあ.

Green pasture, bright sunshine, playful sweets... What a peaceful scene.

We've got a variety of sweets bred now.

The baby chocolates are taking baby steps. They're so cute!

ヒヒーン

NEIGH   BAA BAA   MOO

日本語と同じように、英語でもいくつかの動物の鳴き声の表現は決まっています。mooはウシの「モー」、baaはヒツジの「メー」、neighはウマの「ヒヒーン」です。ニワトリの「コケコッコー」はcock-a-doodle-dooとなります。

75ページ4段目

これも牧場で かおうよ.

今日のおやつは、 シュークリームか.

Let's raise this on the ranch too.

Hmm, today's snack is cream puff.

「シュークリーム」は、英語ではcream puffとなります。日本語の「シュークリーム」は、フランス語のchou à la crèmeからの和製カタカナ語です。

154

83ページ4段目

動詞のwetには、「…を小便でぬらす」という意味があります。94ページの3段目にも、wet my pantsという表現が出てきます。単に「おしっこをもらす」なら、wet oneselfを用いることもできます。

92ページ1段目

「草の根分けても」を、英語では「すべての石（をひっくりかえしてそ）の下をたしかめる」と表現しています。leave no stone unturned（ひっくりかえしていない石はない→できるだけの手をつくす）という慣用表現もあります。

94ページ4段目

「どんな神経してるんだ」を、「鋼鉄の神経をしているにちがいない」と意訳しています。must have iron nervesと言うこともできます。

103ページ2段目

協力するとも. / それが男の友情ってもんだぜ. / 成功させてやろうじゃないか.

> We'll support you.
> That's what male friends are for!
> Let's help him make this work out well.

「それが男の友情ってもんだぜ」を、「男の友達というのはこういうことのためにいるんだ」と意訳しています。

106ページ2段目

そうそう,そうこなくちゃ家出したかいがないよ.

> Yeah yeah, now things are going how I wanted them to.

「そうこなくちゃ家出したかいがないよ」を、「どうやら物事が自分の望んでいたようになってきたぞ」と意訳しています。

122ページ2段目

ああ,ついにカンニングしたか.

> Oh no, are you finally cheating?

cunningという英語はありますが、名詞では「ずるさ、悪知恵」という意味です。「カンニングする」はcheatを使います。「カンニングペーパー」なら、cheat sheetです。

129ページ2段目

まさかきょうのしめきりを、
忘れたんじゃないだろな.

のび太の
ＳＦまんがは？

Don't tell me you forgot that today is the deadline.

What about Nobita's scifi comics?

SFは英語でもそのままSFでつうじますが、scifiもよく使います。SFもscifiも、science fictionを略したものです。

139ページ2段目

どちらさまの, ご婚礼で
ございますか

式場はどこでしょう.

May I have the name of the bride and groom, please?

ATION

Where is the ceremony?

brideは「新婦」、groomは「新郎」のことです。日本語の「新郎新婦」と同じ語順でgroom and brideとしても使いますが、bride and groomの順で使うほうがはるかに多いようです。

146ページ2段目

みちたりた日びの思い出こそ,
きみからの最高のおくり物だったんだよ.

楽しかった日,

それからの毎日,

the memories of contented days,

happy days

After that, every day

those are the greatest gifts you have given us.

場面ごとの断片的なせりふなので、ひとつの文としてはやや不自然なものになっています。After that, every day(…) happy days(…) the memories of contented days, those are the greatest gifts you have given us.と読んでください。

Doraemon ⑧

SHOGAKUKAN ENGLISH COMICS

アートディレクション／海野一雄
カバーデザイン／鈴木麻里子＋ベイブリッジ・スタジオ
カバーイラスト／むぎわらしんたろう ©藤子プロ
英訳・編集協力／(株)ジャレックス
DTP協力／(有)オフィス・エヌ／(株)ニシエ芸
英訳協力／VIZ COMMUNICATIONS INC.
協力／(株)小学館プロダクション
単行本編集責任／山川史郎

2004年4月20日初版第1刷発行　　　　　　　　　（検印廃止）
2007年1月10日　　　第4刷発行

著　者　　藤子・F・不二雄
　　　　　©藤子プロ　2002

発行者　　宮　木　立　雄

印刷所　　文唱堂印刷株式会社
製本所　　株式会社 難波製本　　　PRINTED IN JAPAN

発行所　　（〒101-8001）東京都千代田区一ツ橋二の三の一　株式会社 小学館
　　　　　TEL 販売03(5281)3555 編集03(3230)5685

ISBN4-09-227018-6